U0671082

刘小姐

法图麦·李 著

长江出版传媒 | 长江文艺出版社

扫码收听

想让你听听我的声音，
然后再读这本书。
我觉得挺酷的。
谢谢你愿意花时间读它。

北京长江新世纪文化传媒有限公司
www.cjxinshiji.com
出品

▪ 目 录
CONTENTS

Miss Liu

一

一九三几年的东北，是个满大街都是民生牌汽车的年代。街边又是卖力吆喝的小贩，又是你追我赶的孩子，又是些许管不住手，耸着肩走的小偷以及闲杂人等。人群里，最养眼的，还要数那一个个大脸盘子大眼睛，扭扭搭搭的东北姑娘。

她们头上别着花，身上套着各式各样的旗袍，还时不时露出那么一小段白嫩光滑的大腿。清一色的乌发有的卷着，有的则被摆在耳后。大红色的耳坠、戒指搭配着同样鲜艳的嘴唇，弯弯的柳叶眉在不经意间四处留情，只需一个眼神便能叫那帮大汗淋漓的车夫们丢了魂。

这些人里头，有故事的一大把。

辽宁省本溪市的刘家是个有钱的回族人家。

刘老爷开着一家私人诊所，对中国当时进口的大部分医疗设备都颇有研究，平日里往诊所一待就是好几个时辰。坐诊也好，开药方也罢，反正是谁都拦不住。当时正新鲜的疫苗以及各种其他先进技术，他应有尽有。说好听点，那叫专业。说直接点，他就是一实打实的工作狂。

虽说刘老爷年轻那会也曾叱咤一时，但难得本性纯良，不像他那些个兄弟，满肚子坏水。与他们不同的是，刘老爷打小就乐于助人，为朋友两肋插刀他都是心甘情愿。在他还是个无知的小少爷，整天跟着其他公子哥们在花丛里追蝴蝶时，这个优点就已经开始慢慢显现了。

这些男孩对追姑娘可是颇有心得。闲来无事就上街买几串泛着光的冰糖葫芦，专逗那些个管不住嘴的小姐们。这帮仗着家里有钱有势的富家子弟光靠小打小闹是不能满足的。寻刺激嘛，当然得趁年轻气盛。他们偏偏非得玩过了火，才能从那名叫生命的虚无世界中找到一丝安慰。而跟在后头为他们擦屁股的，自然另有其人。刘老爷曾经对这种行为一贯保持着睁一只眼闭一只眼的态度，只因世道如此，况且他也没少占便宜。不过有那么一桩事，刘老爷到最后都还记忆犹新。

　　他跟他的一发小打俩人都还光着屁股满屋子跑的时候就是邻居了。这发小同样也是蜜罐子里长大的，却不小心惹错了人。据说他看上的那姑娘背景可不简单。别人身后顶多也就有个富家爹爹罩着，可这姑娘竟和当年一唯我独大的黑道人物好上了。这发小可算是赔了夫人又折兵。

　　有天夜里两人正要往家走，却被几个彪形大汉堵了去路。这大半夜的，再怎么喊也不见得能有人来帮忙，更别说一来就撞见这么几位凶神恶煞的索命无常。发小眼看情况不妙，不断督促着让刘老爷先走，他殿后。年纪轻轻的公子哥们就跟大街上那帮毛头小子差不多，都是些没见过什么世面却还要打肿脸充胖子的狗熊。

刘老爷自然是没丢下他，毕竟自己的面子也摆在那呢。只见那帮恶徒中，有一人摸索着掏出了把刀，刘老爷心里顿时凉了半截。这是要玩命啊。他长这么大，还是头一回见敢对着自己掏家伙的人，也不知道上面沾了多少人的心头血。他当即做好了殒命于此的准备，却只听那发小撕心裂肺地喊了一声，那些人就跑了。

刘老爷当时可是心急如焚，只能使劲摁着发小肚子上呼呼冒血的窟窿，也不敢大声呼救，怕把那些人引回来。且想想，一个十指不沾阳春水的小少爷满手是血地跪在地上，眼前还躺着副奄

奄一息的身子。这局面，刘老爷怕是想都没想过
能被自己摊上。

那发小后来因失血过多死了，刘老爷也抑郁了
一段时日。后来再遇见那些个眼波流转却庸脂俗粉
的漂亮姑娘，他也不再动心了。

经这么一折腾，刘老爷也算是领略到了"世事
难料"这四个字的精髓。前一秒还生龙活虎的人，
说没就没了。那阵子过后，他便下定了决心，下半
辈子，一定要医人。

丁氏可同刘老爷从前追过的那些莺莺燕燕不
一样。她从小到大就秉持着一个道理，那就是嫁

得好不如跳得高。像她这样的女人，可是花了刘老爷好大功夫才追到手。

丁氏出身书香门第，父亲和哥哥当年都是名声在外的文化人。家里的女眷虽然没接受过教育，但好歹也对唐诗宋词耳濡目染。去过她家宅子里的人都说，那地方，就连木头柱子都是香的。每每听见这种糊弄小孩的胡话，丁氏不过是一只耳朵进一只耳朵出，只当听戏罢了。

除了父亲跟哥哥，丁氏就没怎么跟其他异性来往过，于是对刘老爷的猛烈追求起初无动于衷。她是偶然听见丫头们议论，说这刘小少爷就跟变了个人似的，竟对自家姑娘如此认真，才动了心的。那也是她唯一一次，破天荒地从头到尾听完了那些闲话。

当时的刘老爷仍然被归类于不是善茬这一栏下，家里有女孩的都提防着他，怕哪天自己闺女也被他始乱终弃。他们不知道的是，本来就没有过多少坏心思的刘老爷，早就已经改过自新，重新做人了。

刘氏夫妇前前后后生了六个男孩、七个女孩，总共十三个孩子。

这么多孩子每天把刘丁氏忙活得够呛，常常恨不得把自己掰成十三瓣，一人分一瓣。最让她头疼的必须是睡觉这件事了。又大又宽的炕上一个个全往中间挤，都想挨着自个妈。最后挨得刘老爷实在受不了，搬到外屋睡去了。小点的挨不着就哭，大点的挨不着就闹，襁褓里的搞不清状况也得跟着叫唤几声。因此刘丁氏经常是两边拍着双胞胎姑娘，脚下躺着几个，身上趴着几个，还有几个就那么生着闷气睡过去的。不知道后来是不是终于想通了，请了位奶妈，这十三块石头，才算是勉强放下了。

要说刘氏夫妇最疼的孩子，那肯定是年龄最小的刘小姐了。作为家里唯一受过教育的女性，刘小姐诗词歌赋样样精通，字还写得极其漂亮。您要是觉得她就是那个年代典型的大家闺秀，那可就大错特错了。刘小姐可不是个一般的女子。她不喜欢脂粉，对漂亮衣裳也没多大兴趣。她更是不信男尊女卑这套不像话的说辞，更不会因此做出任何退让。她一直很清楚自己要什么。一段无忧无虑的童年，一份既稳定又特别的工作，还有一个任凭雨打风吹却仍旧安如磐石的家。

于是她的少女时期，理所应当地轰轰烈烈，刻骨铭心。

***

本溪市另一边，伴着家喻户晓的辽宁民众自卫军军歌和叮叮当当的电车声，黑家那条小狗又开始仰着头汪汪地叫。您还别说，阿岛可真不是条一般的狗。别人家的公鸡打个鸣能把一屋子人吵醒，阿岛一张口，左邻右舍都得从炕上爬起来，冲出去朝着黑家房门吼上那么两三句，解解恨。尤其是夏天的时候，唾沫星子混着汗珠肆意挥洒，楼下路过的偶尔还会伸出手接一下，紧接着撒腿就跑，赶着回家收衣服。

黑家是个产业工人家庭，家里只有黑山这么一个儿子。这要搁到别人家那肯定不是什么好事，但老黑总说，养一个出息的可比养一百个没出息的强。这话邻里听了当然不乐意了。你说得轻巧，那是因为你上辈子不知道积了什么德，落着这么好的孩子。

确实，黑山这小子，从小不哭不闹，还极其懂事。见人知道打招呼，受了别人恩惠知道推辞，推辞不掉知道说声谢谢。这些美德虽然现在听起来不算什么，但在那个走路不小心撞着人都能挨一砖的年代里，黑山这样的，着实少见。

一九四六年，本溪保卫战正式打响。年轻力壮的小伙子们没有一个不去参军，这其中当然也包括一腔热血的黑山。黑家两口子原本是不愿意送黑山走的，毕竟他是家里唯一的孩子，而且才十六，捧在手心里疼还来不及。但老黑眼看着当初怀里牙牙学语的婴孩慢慢长成面前比自己还高半头的年轻人，又顾及到黑山自个的决心，才经过一番心理斗争，艰难地批准了。

为国征战，这是一件多么让人骄傲的事。尽管如此，彼时黑山也才十六岁，这辈子还没遇见过什么大风大浪，对生离死别能有什么概念？

黑山他娘得知这个消息后跟老黑大吵了一架，盘子碗碎了一地。她问老黑，你是不是觉得我特别无私？无私止不了士兵们的鲜血，更换不回他们的命。可那根本没用。深居闺中看不清家国大业，女人的眼泪是那个年代最不值钱的东西。

黑山走的那天下着小雨，老黑就坐在窗边的小桌子旁，平时自己喝酒的地方。临走前他也给黑山倒了一杯，说，虽然有点早，可这画面如果现在看不到，怕以后就没机会了。父子俩之间显然没什么共同话题，只见那两只杯子一次又一次地被饮尽，填满。父亲喝得酩酊大醉，儿子却一直清醒着。

送行的时候老黑没去，据说是喝大了，倒屋里起不来了。黑家的男人不能流眼泪，这是老黑对黑山说的，可他自己却出尔反尔了一回。

略显单薄的少年，身后背着跟自己差不多重的包袱，挥了挥手，就那样云淡风轻地离开了。

二

一九四八年十一月二日，东北解放。

十五岁的刘小姐明眸皓齿，书生意气。

刘小姐是在一个下雪天第一次见到先生的。

他斜顶着军帽，身上披了件墨绿色的呢子大衣，嘴里还叼着支做工精细的红木烟斗。白皙的皮肤倒是不像久经沙场。微挑的双眉下，那对黑玉似的瞳仁缓缓扫过路边的行人。好像如果能有幸被他望见，就是为他挥霍毕生的情爱也不可惜。

这双眼睛，不知道耽误了多少姑娘的青春年华。

刘小姐与先生的第一次对话是烟草味的。

女孩双臂怀抱着一沓书本，冻得有些发红的双手在寒风中略显吃力。一头短发下那张未施粉黛的小圆脸，迎着似有似无的烟雾，紧紧跟随着男人的一举一动。

听说上好的烟草，初次闻是呛鼻的，再一闻是清雅的，而余味则是温润的。

女孩仔细嗅了嗅，是这味道没错了。

男人与女孩对视的瞬间，雪停了。

军靴踏过的地方发出咯吱咯吱的声音。女孩穿着略微潮湿的布鞋静静地立在原地，任凭零零散散的雪花飘落在鞋面上。她的心情无比紧张，对自己体内突如其来的翻江倒海不知该如何是好。于是她就那么站着，直到充斥着鼻腔的烟草味越来越放肆。

男人问道，多大了？

男人又问，叫什么名字？

先生的话是寒冬里的一股暖流，却又好生刺耳。这样温柔的声音，怎么能被卷入那吃人不吐骨头的政治场上呢？但求先生下辈子是个满肚子墨水的教书人，能用他那副嗓子为莘莘学子朗诵诗文。但求他不再被牵扯进那没完没了的明争暗斗，能安安稳稳地娶妻生子，过一世平凡的人生。或许他会有一场盛大的婚礼，又或许两个人的终身会私订在一座隐秘的山林里。他们大概会生三个孩子，两个男孩一个女孩，妹妹被欺负的时候两个哥哥都护着她。他们又或许会就这样一直过下去，膝下无子，做饭砍柴。

那该是多好的一生啊，刘小姐这样想着。

姓刘，十五。

男人默念了一遍女孩的名字，眼里突如其来的深情让人觉得接下来脱口而出的似乎该是另外几个字。他呼出一口气，伸出左手在眼前摆了摆，把方才叼着的烟斗夹在了臂下。取下手套，陶瓷似的手腕，纤长的五根手指，还有发红的指尖，无一不吸引着女孩的视线。

我这样，不妙吧?

***

本溪市税务局，局长办公室。

黑山端坐在办公桌后，有些年头的棕色皮鞋与木质地板融为一体。被太阳晒得黝黑的皮肤，杂乱浓郁的眉，粗糙的指节之间来回游走的钢笔，还有它勉强勾勒出的字。这是阿岛挠的? 惨不忍睹。

面前的姑娘高中毕业，及腰的麻花辫随着她的一举一动左右摇摆，怀表似的看得黑山出了神。漂亮，真漂亮。

叫什么? 黑山问道。

吾恙。

嗯，好名字。回族？

是。

字挺好看。

谢谢。

为什么想当秘书？

想来就来了。

黑山回到家的第一句话就是，爸，我要结婚。老黑这边打着哈欠刚从被窝里钻出来，只听屋子对面正在厨房里忙得热火朝天的黑山他娘大喊一句，选日子！

黑山一把扯下斜挎着的帆布包，着急忙慌地拉开椅子坐了下去。老黑这会儿才逐渐清醒，慢悠悠地也坐了下来。手里鼓捣着的珠子一刻也没停过，就那么盯着自家儿子。也是，都二十一了，再不悸动就有些说不过去了。黑山这块不开窍的木头，作为家里的独苗，老黑还真担心过断后这回事。这几年给他介绍过的对象也是十根指头都数不过来。这不，踏破铁鞋无觅处，得来全不费工夫。黑山这棵铁树，总算是逢春了。

经过一番盘问，老黑也算是大概摸清了对方的底细。同样是回族，长得又标致，还有文化，怎么想都是自己儿子占了便宜。于是英明果断的老黑，当下就接下了黑山让自己去提亲这件差事。

吾姑娘她爹比想象中要直接得多，举手投足间不经意流露出的气质风范唬得老黑一愣一愣的。起初老黑对自己未来亲家的态度完全摸不准，只求别是个自命不凡的主。这一见面才体会到了真正的文质彬彬，有里有面。更让老黑庆幸的是，吾姑娘他爹与自己竟有许多同样的爱好。

老黑这人平时对茶道颇有研究，毕竟上了年纪的人没什么事干，都爱鼓捣这些玩意打发时间。被吾姑娘他爹领着参观茶柜的时候，他一眼就瞧见了自己四处打听都没能讨着的上好龙井。吾姑娘他爹好歹也是个生意人，整日游走在饭局应酬间，察言观色自然不在话下。他将这珍品拿了出来，规规矩矩地开始温具，趁着间隙还偶尔抬眼瞅瞅目不转睛的老黑，在自己心里打着算盘。

看眼前这人这么老实，想必儿子也差不到哪去。再加上黑山在政府工作，两人要是真成了，闺女的下半生也能安稳。至于闺女愿意与否，那就得看黑

山这小子能不能成功俘获她的芳心了，毕竟自己女

儿的主意可大了去了。

几盏茶过后，两位父亲愉快地握住了对方的手，

眼角含笑地达成了共识。

三

一九四九年，中华人民共和国建政。

刘家隔壁的回民饭店每天乌泱泱挤满了人。刘家大院里也没闲着。

用人们左一碗汤，右一盘菜地紧着上，光是看着脚步就让人头晕眼花。刘老爷坐在席中间，一边是刘丁氏，一边是刘小姐，其他子女叽叽喳喳地你一言我一语，好不热闹。姑娘们聊的都是新衣裳、新布鞋。刘家大少爷这边才刚开始跟父亲请教做买卖这回事，没一会就被刘老爷"只赔不赚"四个字打发了。隔壁的老二聚精会神地抱着一本《政治经济学》，还时不时推推鼻梁上不断下滑的眼镜。坐得最远的老三隔三岔五地敲敲桌面，不用问，铁定又是缺了零花钱。饭桌上老四、老五和老六的位子都还留着。刘老爷说了，他们即便是年纪轻轻就不在了，也不能把人家存在过的痕迹抹了去，毕竟曾经都是一家人。

　　刘小姐本性不喜热闹，更别提唠嗑了。这不，筷子一撂，站起来就走。其他人像是见惯了似的，自家老小这脾气，愣是头牛都犟不过她。

　　刘小姐屋内有个衣柜，上好的沉香木做的，费了刘老爷老大劲才给从云南运过来，据说能把衣物催得飘香。起初刘小姐对这柜子的意见可大了去了。占地方不说，还有股奇怪的味，害得她整夜整夜地头疼。不过后来有那么一天，刘小姐放学回家刚好撞见用人们把这柜子往外搬，竟急得亲自上前抱住了它，死活不让动。用人们虽然都有些摸不着头脑，但也没敢继续搬，于是这柜子就这么留下了。

　　这柜子里有个上了锁的红木箱子，打送到刘家起就在那了，愣是在里头摆了几个月才被发现。估计是木匠给买家的一个惊喜，箱子上刻的花纹一看就是功夫活。刘小姐起初本想把它送给刘丁氏的。母亲喜欢用红木箱装首饰，显得人精致大方，可后来却是说什么都不肯给了。

要说这里头都装了些什么，那装的，可是款款深情。

亲爱的兰：

今天你好吗？

昨日看见你放学，本想同你说说话，却见你一脸倦容，便没上前打扰。这段时间没休息好吧？我知道你学业繁忙，却没想到如此费神。自那天遇见你之后，我便满脑子都是你。虽然这样说话有些唐突，可我偏是不可控地想着你。近来天冷，多喝些热水暖暖胃，可别感冒。你要是愿意，就上你们学校对面的饭馆里坐坐吧。要说我没私心那是假的，不过想让你尝尝他们家的糖饼是真的。我听说小姑娘家都好吃甜食，不知道你喜不喜欢？

　　盼安。

亲爱的兰：

　　今天你好吗？

　　记得前两天答应过要带你去湖边走走，不知道你何时方便？你父亲管得严，要是不行也无妨。只是几日不见，有些想你罢了。最难的时候已经过去了，我倒是有些不务正业，整天借着写诗打发时间。下次见面我想送你几首我新写的，一是请你帮忙品品，二是希望你也能惦记着我。我等你答复。

　　盼安。

亲爱的兰：

今天你好吗？

今天早晨路过你家院子，在门口看见了几枝你最喜欢的榆叶梅。你说它有欣欣向荣的意味，我平时虽然对这些不太了解，不过你说的，想必都是对的。改天我也在我住处附近种上两棵，随你一起进步。我还想找个空旷些的地方，种上一大片，等来年四五月份的时候同你一起去赏花，你看如何？

盼安。

＊＊＊

一九五一年冬天。

这一天，黑山难得起得比阿岛还早。他着急忙慌地跳下了炕，一路小跑着进了外头的公共便所，身后带上的门发出了结结实实的一声响，直接震醒了老黑两口子。

心气不顺的老黑刚要追出去撒撒火，就被老伴一把拉了回来。他嘟囔了几句只有自己听得见的话，随后又转身倒下了。只是这么一闹，黑山他娘倒是再也睡不着了。毕竟今天是个大日子，她可得给自己儿子好好做顿早饭，壮壮士气。正琢磨着该做些什么好，就听见了平日里同自己还算亲近的邻居张婶洪亮的嗓音。

张婶这人特别热心肠，黑家偶尔有什么需要她都尽可能地照应着。知道他们家是回民，所以请他

们吃饭时，桌上摆的绝对一律清真。不过这热心肠
倒不仅仅是为了友好的邻里关系，而是因为那张婶
家里有个还算标致的小侄女，从小就对男子气概十
足的黑山万分景仰。张婶原先无数次找黑山他娘聊
天的目的，都是为了能让自己侄女跟黑山处对象，
甚至把将来俩人结婚之后到谁家拜年的顺序都构思
了一遍。

　　黑山他娘虽说对张婶没什么意见，对她家那小
侄女也还算认可，但她总觉得差了点什么，于是每
次都巧妙地避开了这个话题。日子久了，张婶见自
己侄女明显是一厢情愿，倒也没再过多地提起这件
事。只是这天，不知是谁走漏了风声，让她直接找
上了黑家的门。

　　虽说交谈到最后两人不欢而散，可黑山他娘却

因为把事情挑明了，总算松了口气。强扭的瓜不甜这道理，她可是再清楚不过了。想当年自己与老黑，那也是久经坎坷才好不容易修成了正果。只不过毕竟是做母亲的，她也有些心疼张家那小侄女，一片真心到最后却什么也不是。

后来那小侄女嫁了个官二代，是个整天好吃懒做的主。那人似乎性格也不怎么样，稍微提高点嗓门跟他争上几句他就动手。那天黑山出门前这小侄女去找他了。常听别人说，将死之人都会回光返照，她对黑山的执着好像也是这样。豆蔻年华的少女，遇到了一个承载着所有美好的人。如果可以的话，她当然会继续等，只因为他是光，触不可及，又耀眼到让人无法回避。当所有对爱情的憧憬和幻想都摆在眼前，有谁会掉头再去追求别的东西？可唯独感情这玩意，能一次又一次地给予伤害，让最执着的人选择离开。

她不擅长说话，动不动就害羞，不是黑山喜欢的类型。她很清楚这一点，可她不想再懦弱了。她就是想拼一次，也算是给自己这么多年来偷偷红过的脸一个交代。她准备了一大段说辞，可真正站到黑山面前的时候她却又害怕了。她怕被拒绝，更怕被拒绝后自己会从他的生命里消失。

她对黑山最后的印象是一个仓促的微笑。明明是那么阳光的人，却总对自己疏离得过分。是啊，他要去追求他喜欢的姑娘了，可千万别把他临走前的礼貌当作救命稻草。除了祝福，自己好像并没有什么能拿得出手的。路上小心，她说。尽管这最后一个字，连同她最后残存的一丝希望，都被黑山离开时带起的风刮走了。

再怎么怕疼，也得撞一回南墙。

听别人说那小侄女嫁过去没多久就死于非命，而她那官二代丈夫则娶了同他一起长大的青梅，连灵牌都没能摆进夫家的祠堂。

自古红颜多薄命，说得还真没错。

黑山从便所回来以后借过他娘的镜子仔细研究了一番自己的脸。他的五官绝对不次，眉眼中透露出的英气，少说也能迷倒些初出茅庐的小姑娘，但偏偏今天让他怎么都看不顺眼。一会觉得黑眼圈太重了，跟只熊猫似的，一会又觉得眼睛里的血丝太明显了，一看就像休息不好，肾虚的症状。总之，黑山的早晨是伴着阿岛的叫声，他娘的唠叨声，和自己逐渐加快的心跳声一块度过的。

因为今天，是他和吾恙的第一次约会。

黑山听老黑说，姑娘家都喜欢逛街。对恋爱约会这方面毫无经验的他，虽然对老黑的提议疑心满满，但除了硬着头皮照做，还真是没有更好的法子。黑山家里有些拮据，坐电车的钱凑了一个星期都没凑齐。他本来想着在附近溜达溜达，看看景就挺好的了。至于逛街，应该跟遛弯没什么差别吧？

吾恙主动掏了来回的车票钱，这一大公无私的举动，使她在黑山心里的地位又光辉伟大了许多。

黑山从没见过像她一样，从眉眼到举动都透露着清冷的姑娘，跟自己从前那些只会受人摆布的相亲对象简直是天差地别。任何物件在她眼里都激不起丝毫水花，反倒是黑山担心那些东西玷污了它们的纯净。偶尔，当这双眼睛停留在某枝花、某棵树上的时候，黑山仿佛能看见它们的变化，却怎么也想不出这变化的缘由。每到那个时候，黑山就告诉自己，等他赚够了钱，第一件事就是娶她。到时候，酒席一定要办得大张旗鼓，让所有人都知道，这吾姑娘，进了他黑家的门。

四

刘小姐十六岁那年学会了抽烟。

她为此被刘丁氏数落了不知道多少回，说她一回族姑娘整天手里拿着支烟斗，一点都不像话。刘小姐倒是从没把这些放在心上，总趁自己母亲说得口干舌燥到处找茶喝的工夫继续抽，不以为然。

抽烟是她那年冬天学会的。想必刘小姐与先生的初见在她心里留下了浓重的一笔，以至于每回下雪的时候，她都拿着烟斗坐在炕上，朝着窗外小片小片的雪花呼气。刘小姐抽烟的时候极漂亮。轻颤着的睫毛和潮红的双颊，都彰显着她时而波涛汹涌，时而静如止水的思绪。也唯有她才能把烟抽得如此雅致了吧。

都说刘小姐秀外慧中，谁要是娶了她那可真是烧了高香了。但她独自一人的时候却经常会想，如果自己是个男人会是什么样？"他"该是个学富五车的知识分子。眉清目秀，但不是个专情的人。即便片叶不沾身，也不会有人责骂，因为他们都相信"他"会带来改变，带领所有人走向更好的未来。而被"他"玩弄过的女人，都不过会成为"他"谈笑风生时拿来打趣的话柄。

　　刘小姐已经有些天没收到过先生的书信了。自己父亲对先生的态度她看得一清二楚，只不过是不想捅破这层纸，不然就真的连一丝念想都没了。但热恋中的年轻男女哪顾得上这些啊？就是三天不见都想得慌，何况这俩人已经几个星期没来往了。刘老爷绞尽脑汁想出了无数种理由阻止她出门，可刘小姐这刚烈的性子哪受得了这样的束缚？在又一次出逃失败之后，刘老爷终于发怒了。

　　刘老爷虽算不上什么严父，却也是个明白人。刘小姐每天夜里偷偷往外跑这件事他早就知道了。之所以没草率地做出什么大动作是因为好奇，到底是什么样的人，能把自家闺女这般性子冷淡，高高在上的小姑娘迷得神魂颠倒。

　　人都是护犊的，更别提像刘老爷这般偏心的父亲了。虽说在那个年代，十六岁也到了该谈婚论嫁的年纪，可他就是对这来路不明、神神秘秘的先生喜欢不起来。再往深了一打听，好家伙，是个汉民！绝对不行。

　　先生住所隔壁的小巷子是他们的秘密花园。虽然跟刘家大院有段距离，可刘小姐却丝毫不在乎。刘丁氏跟她说过，这世上有两种爱情。第一种是奋不顾身的，等到哪天你真的爱上了一个人，就是叫你跋山涉水你也心甘情愿。而第二种是细水长流的，是柴米油盐，是小打小闹，却也是最踏实的。我想着你大概更向往第一种，因为那样的体验只能有一次，可它不够长久。

　　姑娘家，要是想落得下半生安稳，还是该选第二种。

　　刘小姐时常会想起刘丁氏的话，然后剩下的就只有不屑。打出生起，她就知道自己跟别人不一样。她是那花丛中开得最美的一朵，却也是刺最多最尖的。她相信爱情本就该轰轰烈烈，就算不知道接下来要往哪走，起码以后回想起来是与众不同的。

　　刘小姐跟先生在一起的时候最喜欢看先生抽烟。她自己也不明白，为什么别人抽烟让她厌恶，而先生抽烟却让她着迷。先生偶尔会俯下身来在刘小姐耳边轻轻呼出一口含着些许烟雾的气，不经意的动作磨得人魂牵梦绕。

　　他会蛊惑人心。

刘小姐说想学抽烟，可想而知地遭到了反对。她问为什么，先生只用一句对身体不好打发了。先生又问她怎么净喜欢这些乱七八糟的东西，于是刘小姐就义正词严地列出了自己不喜欢的所有事物。她不喜欢的东西真的很多，多到数都数不过来。

那会不会有一天，你连我也不喜欢了？
瞎说，我只喜欢你。

先生说，如果可以，他希望自己能死在战场上，因为那是离他的信仰最近的地方。他不想一辈子靠头脑过活，时而日复一日，时而无所事事的生活早就把他的耐心磨尽了。那些明枪暗箭，那些钩心斗角，统统都去一边吧！他真正想做的，是拿起把枪。

先生死在了一九四九年的秋天。

枯黄的叶子落在他的头上、身上，是他浑身上下最显眼的颜色。后来先生还是没能种下那片榆叶梅，甚至没能等到来年春夏交替，那花开得最好看的时候。他没能如自己所希望的那般死在战场上，而他在这世上留下的最后一眼里，有参差不齐的瓦房，有黑压压的头顶，却唯独没有刘小姐的影子。围观的人群散去后的场景，何其凄凉。曾经那么爱干净的人，就这样散于秋风中，葬于泥土里。

刘小姐是真心想过嫁给先生，也相信先生是真心想过要娶自己回家。

＊＊＊

一九五八年，黑山二十八，吾恙二十五。

吾恙她爹已经公私合营了自己的诊所，金圆券全部作废，成了每个月拿着八百块钱的闲人。他起初还有些舍不得，那诊所可是他倾尽心力做起来的，说放手谈何容易？可转念一想，这反倒是件好事。毕竟单凭自己这几十年来积攒的丰厚家底，以及明显不及当年的身子骨，也到了该享享清福的时候了。本想着能被自己闺女孝敬孝敬，可还没过几年，吾恙跟黑山这对夫妇就搬去了宁夏。

在这之前，吾恙可是位实打实的职业女性。她嫁给黑山后离开了自己出生的城市，父亲随他搬到了长春。作为长春电影制片厂的电影剪辑师，她剪辑过无数部作品，这其中就包括当时家喻户晓的《大河奔流》。吾恙当初选择做这行也不是没原因的。她对影片里那些感天动地的爱情故事兴趣极大。明明能把大部分桥段里的对白背得滚瓜烂熟，却在别人问起的时候粗略带过，硬说自己忘了。说她脸皮薄也好，小家碧玉也罢，那都是不了解她的人才会做出的草率结论。吾恙不想说的话、不想干的事，就是玉皇大帝下凡都只能抓耳挠腮，无计可施。就这样，她在剪辑的过程中，以旁观者的身份，默默地体验着别人的人生。

原本平淡的日子却因为黑山被升为交际处处长

发生了变化。跟着他搬到宁夏回族自治区的吾恙由于没有对口单位，只能放弃原先的专业。承载着优秀知识女性独立坚强的性格以及那股不甘心的劲，她最终选择了进入宁夏京剧团，并且直接成为了人事干部。

看的戏越多，吾恙越能感受到，其实电影跟京剧同样都是一个道理。它们都在讲故事。它们最大的差别，无非是一个戏在人中戏不知，而另一个是人在戏中人不知。吾恙经常会想，虞姬那两把剑，到底是舞给霸王，还是舞给自己？那一声"大王"，是痛下决心，还是心灰意冷？项羽这等骁勇善战的一国之首，即便是杀出了重围，最后还不是以无颜面对江东父老为由随虞姬去了？可见一个人，是君也好是臣也罢，绝不能丢了这漫漫一生中最宝贵的东西，管它是江山还是美人。

　　经历这么多，吾恙却还是幸福的。黑山对她的照顾无微不至，对她的理想也是尽可能地配合。要是两人在外头有饭局，吾恙弱弱的一声累了，黑山绝对是毫不犹豫地买完单就带着媳妇回家。他那帮狐朋狗友还经常抱怨，说什么这结个婚，竟连自由都没了？黑山也是听听就罢，毕竟他们不是自己，这其中鼬甜的滋味他们哪能懂啊？

　　虽说黑山在艺术赏识这方面明显次于吾恙，可他为了能同自家媳妇时不时来上一段有深度的对话下了不少功夫。一本本京剧史录早就被他翻得破烂不堪，上面花花绿绿的全是笔记。黑山偶尔也会纳闷，吾恙脑子里这些想法到底是从哪来的，平时也没见她读过什么哲学类的书啊。可越是这样，黑山越觉得吾恙真的是个很特别的人。究竟哪一点特别倒也说不上来，他就是感觉自己这辈子，不会再遇到另一个和她接近的了。

伴着傲人智慧的，是萦绕着吾恙的大小姐习性。她嫁过去以后可是无比地快活。从小养尊处优的吾恙什么活都不干，也不会干。顶多在家磕嗑瓜子，上上班，跟街坊邻居打打麻将。在宁夏待了几年之后，她的麻将技术连身经百战的京剧团团长都自愧不如。

吾恙早上起床第一件事就是喝茶，还必须得是热乎的青稞茶。黑山作为局长，巴结他的人数不胜数。每当黑山提着大包小包回到家时，吾恙总是对那帮浑身烟酒味的人送的俗茶嗤之以鼻。吾恙最不喜欢跟别人一样，而黑山爱的偏生就是她这娇而不作的性子，于是每天兢兢业业地，天还没亮就起床，算着时间仔细把茶给沏好，生怕放久了变凉，沏晚了又太烫。

这样平静舒坦的日子，吾恙自有记忆起就想象过了。

五

一九五一年年初，刘小姐成年。

刘家二小姐因肺结核病死。

刘小姐几次质问过刘老爷，明明从前开过诊所，手里有的是救命的家伙，为什么不管二姐。刘老爷次次重复的都是同一句话，嫁出去的女儿，泼出去的水。想想也是讽刺，当年风风光光出嫁的堂堂刘

家二小姐，竟落得这般下场。刘小姐还依稀记得她
嫁人前一夜，拉着自己说了十几年来都未曾说过的
掏心窝子话。二姐千叮咛万嘱咐，让她好好照顾刘
丁氏，说母亲身体不好，得尽量少动换。随后又一
个不落地问候了刘家上下好几口子人。刘小姐一边
点着头答应，一边观察着二姐的神情，丝毫不像个
即将嫁人的新娘子。

　　姐。

　　嗯？

　　你爱他吗？

　　刘二小姐说了，她的夫婿家世好，有文化，能
嫁过去是她的福分。更何况，爱情这东西，再怎么

轰轰烈烈，死后能带走吗？她表面上看得再开，刘
小姐也一眼就能看透。即将嫁给心爱之人的姑娘怎
么会流眼泪？她偏偏就是看准了，自家二姐流的眼
泪，跟随处张贴的喜字一点都搭不着边。

刘二小姐心里明白，这个男尊女卑的世界从来
没有公平可言。她很羡慕刘小姐，从小就被父亲
和家人宠大，半分苦头都没吃过。刘老爷除了一
手包办自家几个儿子的衣食住行，唯一还照顾着，
生怕磕了碰了的就是刘小姐了。刘老爷经常语重
心长地摸着她的手，嘴里嘟囔着"老疙瘩"、"我
们老疙瘩"之类的话。刘二小姐倒也是心大，把
自己父亲明显的偏心只当作是操心罢了，就这样
放在心里还算好过。

她出嫁那天换上了一脸的虚情假意，旁人根本看不出，只当她是开心坏了。亮红色的布景衬得刘二小姐容光焕发，任谁家姑娘看了都会羡慕她这般声势浩大的婚礼。

刘小姐记得二姐跟二姐夫登记结婚那天，二姐从左顾右盼到怅然若失的神情。她今天看着二位新人拜堂的时候好像明白了些什么。

感情这东西说不清道不明，不定什么时候觉着对了就是对了。

刘小姐曾经与那男子有过一面之缘，是在家跟二姐学做针线活时碰见的。也不知道当时是着了什么魔，竟以为自己能给先生亲手做件衣裳。可谁知道，这东西还没送出去呢，人就没了。

那男子当时手里抱着盆不知名的多肉类植物，人还算精神。论不上惊为天人，却是那种能让人安下心来与他谈天说地的类型。想必刘二小姐后来对花花草草的关心应该也是从他这得来的。对了，他名唤阿六，也是个回民。中产家庭，父亲好像是个老师，想来跟刘小姐多半是打过照面。自二小姐结婚那天起他就再没出现过，管他是参军了还是把家搬到别地去了，总之这两个人是不会再见了。

人真的很奇怪，总是把不能拥有的当作是最好的。

二小姐下葬那天，刘小姐听着阿訇沉甸甸的声音，琢磨透了一个道理。不管你生前是富贵还是贫穷，被万人敬仰还是受尽唾弃，死后都是形单影只。二小姐在世时最喜爱的布鞋留下了，最宝贝的玉镯子留下了，最尽心尽力服侍的男人也在短暂的悲伤过后另觅良人了。

二小姐的丈夫虽然不是个完美的男人，可刘小姐却有些心疼他。许是因为两个人的经历或多或少有些相似，刘小姐在他后来的婚礼上还读了首自己写的诗，大致意思是祝二位新人白头到老。她希望二姐给不了的，另一个人能给他，因为这个男人一定也有很多难处，他的人生也早就不能用一帆风顺来形容了。延续香火的重担都压在他一人身上，对两个家庭的结合没有选择权的也一定不只二姐一个。

刘小姐在喜宴上陪他说了许多话。

老妹，你看啊。我俩结婚的时候她二十三，我二十九，差了六岁。她走的时候才二十四，我正好三十。我今年三十二，又结婚了，她还是二十四。我以后生了孩子她二十四，抱了孙子她二十四，我要是有那四世同堂的福气她也是二十四。到我死那天，我怎么也得七八十了，她还是二十四。

二十四岁，是永远刚刚好的年纪和年轻靓丽的皮囊，是从此以后在别人脑海里浮现时她唯一的模样。

年初的天气还是冷的，在外头待久了也还是会

止不住地打战。二小姐生前养的那朵扶桑花，竟在
她去世当天才微微张开，到她下葬这天那没良心的
便已经开得明艳动人。

＊＊＊

　　吾恙二十七岁那年，母亲去世了。

　　同年，大姑娘出生了。

　　大姑娘的到来好像是专门为了慰藉吾恙似的。
初为人母，她对一切都非常陌生。本指望着母亲能
帮上些忙，造化却总是弄人。吾恙母亲走得干净，
没受多少苦，但越是这样她越自责。吾恙总觉得自
己这一生亏欠母亲的太多，年轻时让她太过操心，

才导致她晚年时身体状态一天不如一天。本该替家里人好好照顾她，却还是没能把她留下来。

母亲走后近一个月的时间里，吾恙满脑子都是一位故人说过的话。她紧紧握着自己的手，恳切地说过的掏心窝子话。

我们生在这世上，什么也带不来，什么也带不走。走完这一遭，圆满也好，遗憾也罢，总归是走过了。

吾恙就是想着这些，才能在收拾母亲遗物的时候感到心安。

大姑娘的啼哭声总是能让心情低落的吾恙重新

振作起来。不管发生什么，日子还得过。吾恙虽说不是个吃苦耐劳的主，但关键时刻却总是能勇敢得不像话。她每天全心全意地照顾大姑娘，一点点模仿着母亲对自己的养育过程。她坚信，既然母亲能够养出自己这样看似不怎么合群，内心却充满了大道理的孩子，那她也一定可以。

有些夜里，在吾恙哄大姑娘睡觉的时候，她仿佛能从孩子澄亮的眼睛里看到母亲的影子。

吾恙三十六岁那年，父亲去世了。

同年，小姑娘出生了。

父亲去世之前给了吾恙一副棉手闷子，里面有张八百块钱的存折。这老滑头，临了了还惦记着给自己的小闺女留下点什么。

老爷子走之前跟她说了许多话，其中大部分是关于吾恙年轻时候的事。父亲自认有些对不起她。虽说她现在有了自己的家庭，还有份稳定的工作，但他却怎么都忘不了吾恙在老宅子里歇斯底里的那副样子。那是他闭上眼睛都能看见的画面。吾恙每回听到这些，总会拿一切都过去了这样的话来安慰父亲。其实过没过去她心里有数，少女时期发生过的事，哪那么容易忘记？可她早就说服了自己，人的一生不可能十全十美。再干净的东西，也会在经历时间的沉淀后变得灰头土脸，面目全非。

吾恙面对父亲的离开要比母亲那次从容得多。大姑娘已经九岁了，绝大部分时间都能自娱自乐。

小姑娘虽然刚出生，却不哭不闹，乖得很。这让她省了很大的心，能够一丝不苟地安排父亲的后事。

父亲的离开就好像是吾恙前半生的结尾，带走的不仅仅是对曾经那个家的念想，还有自己这么多年来心里一直解不开的结。

从那天起，吾恙十八岁以前的日子就像是自己剪辑过的那些影片一样，恍如隔世。

六

黑山终年六十七。

人们都说他这辈子很圆满。娶了个漂亮的回族姑娘，还生了两个乖巧伶俐的女儿。

黑山像是知道自己要走了，于是在最后的时日里默默打点好了一切。已经嫁人了的两个女儿对他的病情一无所知，整天只见他乐乐呵呵地，怎么看都不像是身子骨有毛病的人。黑山唯一的遗憾，就是没能抱着小姑娘给自己生的外孙女。除此之外，他对自己这朴实无华的一生倒也再无渴求。黑山临走前同吾恙说了许多话，在这就不一一告知了。只是猜就能猜得到，这个让他用尽了几十年情爱的女人，他自然是要好好道别。

　　回想黑山这辈子所遇见过的人和事，只能用平凡两个字形容。平凡的出身，平凡的初恋，平凡地成家，平凡地离去。可就是这样一个平凡的人做到了一心一意地付出，从未图过任何回报。他明白人生是短暂的，也懂得去珍惜该珍惜的人。他也从没抱怨过时光仓促，因为六十七个年头已经足够让他认清这些道理。他因别人的幸福而幸福，他的一生从来不是为了自己而活。

　　有了担当的两个女儿确保了黑山走得体面，同时还留意着吾恙的情绪，而她却总是让孩子们去忙活别的，说自己年纪大了，不喜欢热闹。这句话不掺半点真心。吾恙这辈子觉得最幸福的事就是女儿们在自己身边说说笑笑，坚强了一辈子的她只是不知道该怎样面对这样突如其来的失去。她这一生失去过很多东西，也自认对失去这项危险的运动驾轻就熟。吾恙只是没有想到，兜兜转转这么些年，她竟然还能体会到第一次般的痛苦，甚至更烈。

　　黑山来的时候一无所有，可他走时却带走了吾恙全部的爱。

吾恙不抽烟已经很多年了。唯独黑山走的那天，她背着孩子们偷偷买了一包。生涩地将烟点燃，随后把另一头搁在嘴里，上下牙之间。

时间的流逝改变了很多东西。从战乱到和平，吾恙都体会了一遍。眼看着曾经的一切被推翻、重建，唯一没变的，是她从未停滞不前的心。她要跟上时代的变化，也要遵从自己内心的改变。

没了烟斗倒还挺好，她本就觉得笨重，这下果真轻松多了。

吾恙那天晚上独自一人躺在床上时并没有不习惯，只是对充斥着鼻腔的烟味有些不满。黑山曾经说过，女人不该抽烟，就该每天香喷喷地被男人养着。吾恙当时还跟他大吵了一架，吓得黑山不知该如何是好，只能像从前一样低头认错。毕竟在吾恙面前，黑山再不是那个顶天立地的男子汉，而是服服帖帖的好男人。现在想想，她也被当时的自己逗乐了。她自然明白黑山的意思，那颗总是想着讨好自己的心，是藏也藏不住的。

多少次吾恙告诉自己，想哭就哭吧。别慌，黑山只是去了一个更好的地方。他太累了，你要学会放手，要笑着送他走，要告诉他，没关系，有我呢。但太阳还会升起，夜晚还会降临。你要在孤立无助的时候想起他，然后下定决心，活成他如果还在的话你曾经幻想过的自己的模样。等那副模样彻彻底底地渗入皮肤，融入血液，沉入你与他大同小异的白骨。是了，你要将它融入骨血。在那之后你要开始新的生活。你要嗑瓜子，打麻将。看日出，看日落。

　　她对自己说，你要活得比从前更好，因为他在等你，等一切尘埃落定后只有你们两个人的日子。

七

妈，你一开始看上老头了吗？

人长得挺精神，就是家里太穷。

那妈，你有初恋吗？

没有。

黑山笑了笑，怎么没有？以前有个很帅的国民

党军官追你妈。

国民党怎么就没成呢？这个男的最后去哪了？

不知道。

黑山又笑了笑，你猜他最后上哪去了？

是撤退到台湾了，还是被俘虏了？

被毙了。

妈，你叫吾恙，可是姥爷姓刘，你为什么不

叫刘吾恙？

张王李赵遍地刘，姓刘的人太多了。

我不愿做那大多数。

MISS LIU

one

The Northeast in the 1930s had its streets packed with Min Sheng automobiles, the most popular brand at the time. There were peddlers, thieves, and children chasing after each other. All kinds of people roamed the place. But the Northeastern girls, with their bright faces, bright eyes, and the delicate swaying of their hips, were always the center of attention.

They wore flowers on their heads and Qi Paos that exposed a decent portion of their smooth, pale thighs. Some had their dark hair curled, and some preferred to tuck them behind their ears, letting them flow down their shoulders like waterfalls. Bright red jewelry and lips of the same color moved up and down as they chattered away, and eyebrows shaped like willow leaves on a warm April day flirted unintentionally. Just one glance would leave the coachmen dazed, wishing they could be right beside them.

These people, they have all kinds of stories.

The Lius from Ben Xi city, located in the Liaoning province, were a wealthy Hui family.

Master Liu owned a private clinic and knew his way around most of the medical equipment and new vaccines imported to China during that time. He would stay there for hours on end, seeing patients and prescribing medicine with such enthusiasm that no one seemed to be able to pull him away from his work.

An extremely passionate man.

Although Master Liu did experience a rebellious phase when he was a teenager, he had still been a nice kid on the inside. Unlike his brothers and friends, he had always enjoyed helping others, even strangers. It was difficult for people to understand why he acted that way. He was rich and the youngest son of a prestigious family, kindness was the last thing he needed.

The boys he hung out with, on the other hand, were nothing but trouble. They found pursuing girls especially fascinating. They would buy sugarcoated haws put on sticks off the streets and tease the girls with a big appetite. They never had to worry about dealing with the consequences, because they were young, rich, and they knew that someone else would be there to tidy up the mess they've made. Master Liu didn't join them, but he didn't call them out either. That's how the world works, he would tell himself. It was true. That was how the world worked.

Although there was this one incident that Master Liu could never forget.

He had a dear friend. The two grew up together, from diapers to girls, they were practically inseparable. Wealthy and good-looking, the two of them didn't have a care in the world. But things quickly took a turn from there.

Apparently, the girl his friend had messed with was the mistress of a gang leader.

One night, Master Liu and his friend

were on their way home when several sturdy men surrounded them. They knew who these men were, and they knew that escaping was going to be hard, if possible at all. Master Liu's friend, being the reason why their lives were in danger, told him to leave and that he would handle the rest. It wasn't funny back then, but it is now. How was he, a slim and spoiled young master, going to knock these guys down? But he couldn't bear with the thought of losing face.

What's the difference between him and the beggar boys on the streets? Both inexperienced, both impulsive, and both incapable of surrendering their egos.

Of course, Master Liu didn't listen. He had his own pride to feed.

He immediately regretted his decision to stay when he saw one of the men draw out a knife. All he could think about was how many people it had killed. The blood, the screaming, the begging for mercy. He was ready to die. He had prepared himself for the worst, and he was sure that this was the end.

He heard his friend let out a shrill cry, and footsteps shuffling further and further away.

Master Liu was desperate. All he could do was press down on the gaping hole in his friend, too scared to make a sound. Try picturing a shivering rich young master on top of a seemingly lifeless body.

Master Liu had never imagined this happening to him.

His friend died later due to excessive blood loss. Master Liu became depressed for a while, and no longer cared about chasing after pretty girls.

After this incident, Master Liu finally learned how unpredictable the world is. The person standing in front of you right now could be gone in the next second. From that very moment, he made a decision to heal the wounded and treat the dying for the rest of his life.

Miss Ding was not like most girls. The one single principle she had been upholding since childhood was that, a higher social status is always better than a powerful bonding marriage. It took Master Liu a lot of effort to pursue her.

Miss Ding was born into an educated family. Her father and brother were both well known for being knowledgeable scholars. Although the women in her family never went to school, they were at least familiar with ancient poetry and archaism. Those who had been to her house would say that even the wooden pillars smelled like knowledge. Whenever Miss Ding heard such nonsense, she would pretend as if she was listening to a horribly performed opera.

Apart from her father and brother, Miss Ding had never really interacted with other men, so at first, she was unimpressed by Master Liu's pursuit. Until one day, she accidentally eavesdropped on her maidservants talking about how Master Liu had changed into a completely different person since he had never tried this hard to win a girl over. That was the first time she stood there and finished listening to a conversation that would normally sound like nothing but a joke to her.

At the time, Master Liu was still considered trouble. Families with daughters kept them away from him, for fear that he would eventually abandon them. What they didn't know was that Master Liu had always been a decent young man, and the last bit of rebelliousness in him had already been washed away by his experiences.

The Lius gave birth to six boys and seven girls, thirteen in total.

Mrs. Liu, née Ding, struggled with taking care of all her children, especially when it was bedtime. They would all try to push their way past each other to reach the center of the kang so they could sleep right next to their mother. Master Liu couldn't take it anymore and eventually moved to the living room. The younger ones would cry, the older ones would yell, and the babies who didn't know what was going on would also chime in. In the end, Mrs. Liu, née Ding, would have kids lying next to her arms, her feet, on top of her, and with their backs turned against her because they didn't get a good spot. Maybe she finally thought the whole thing through, so she hired a nanny, and took the pressure off her shoulders.

The Lius loved their youngest daughter the most. As the only educated woman in her family, Miss Liu excelled at both reading and writing. She was extremely smart, and her handwriting was exceptional. Miss Liu wasn't a typical young lady from a well-to-do family, and she wasn't just another pretty face. She didn't like rouge and powder, she wasn't interested in new clothes, and she didn't believe in female inferiority. She always knew what she wanted. A carefree childhood, a stable yet unordinary job, and a family of her own that nothing could break apart.

Her teenage years, of course, were passionate, intense, and memorable.

***

On the other side of the city, accompanied by the Liaoning People's Self-Defense Army Song and the ringing of a nearby tram, the Hei family's dog began barking again. You see, A Dao wasn't just any dog. Roosters crow and they wake an entire room. When A Dao barked, even the neighbors would scramble up from their kangs and rush outside, just to yell at the Hei family's door. Especially during the summer, spit and sweat would mix together and sprinkle down. Those who happened to be walking by would raise a hand up, then run back home to collect their clothes that had been drying outside.

The Heis were industrial workers, and Hei Shan was the only son. This would be tragic to any other family, but Hei Shan's father always said that raising one good one is always better than raising a hundred bad ones. Of course, the neighbors were mad. Hei Shan's father made it sound so easy because Hei Shan was a great boy.

Hei Shan rarely cried or caused trouble, and he was very sensible. He knew he had to say hello to familiar faces, politely turn down gifts from others, and when he couldn't, say thank you. They don't sound like much these days, but back then, in a society where you'd get smacked by a brick if you bumped into someone on the street, people like Hei Shan weren't everywhere.

In 1946, The War of Defense in Ben Xi had officially begun. Boys who were young and strong all chose to enlist, including Hei Shan. At first, Hei Shan's parents didn't want to send him away. He was their only child, and only sixteen years old. He was supposed to be protected and cared for.

But when Hei Shan, who was no longer a baby but an ardent young man taller than he was, stood there looking into his eyes, Hei Shan's father gave his permission.

Fighting for your country is a noble deed. However, Hei Shan was only sixteen. He had never faced a single challenge by himself, how much would he know about life and death?

When Hei Shan's mother found out about the enlistment, she and Hei Shan's father had their biggest argument. Dishes and bowls were shattered on the floor. She asked her husband if he thought she was really selfless. Being selfless was not going to put a stop to the bloodshed, or save the lives of the soldiers. But it was pointless. Women were told that they couldn't understand politics, and their tears were the cheapest item of all.

It rained the day Hei Shan left. His father sat right next to the little tea table near the window, where he usually drank. He poured Hei Shan a drink before he left, and said, although it's a bit early, I'm afraid that I'll never be able to do this again. The two obviously didn't have a topic of conversation, only the glasses were emptied and filled, over and over. Hei Shan's father was completely wasted, while Hei Shan remained calm and collected.

Hei Shan's father wasn't there to send him away. He was too drunk to stand up and was sleeping like a baby. Us men from the Hei family, he used to say to Hei Shan, we don't cry. But he didn't stick to his words.

A frail-looking boy, with a bundle almost the size of himself, waved gently and left.

two

November 2nd, 1948. Northeast Liberation.

Fifteen-year-old Miss Liu had a pair of bright eyes and the mind of an educated woman.

It was snowing the first time she met

Mister.

A soldier hat sat tilted on his head, a dark green woolen overcoat draped over his body, and between his lips, a delicately-crafted mahogany pipe. His skin was fair, it didn't seem like he fought on the front line. Under his slightly raised eyebrows, eyes that resembled two pieces of gleaming jet swept across the people walking by. It almost felt like if his eyes happened to land on you, you'd be willing to squander all of your love and affection for him.

Those eyes, I wonder how many young girls fell for them during the best years of their lives.

The first conversation between Miss Liu and Mister smelled like tobacco.

Her arms were wrapped around a stack of books, and her fingers had turned red in the biting wind. She had short hair and a clear, round face that followed his movements in the faint smoke.

Some people say that good tobacco smells acrid at first, then refined, and finally, gentle.

She took another sniff. It seemed about right.

The snow stopped when he looked at her.

His military boots made a crackling sound as he trod forward. Her damp cloth shoes stayed put as tiny specks of snowflakes melted on top of them. She was nervous. She didn't know what was happening to her, so she stood there until the smell of tobacco became more and more distinct.

How old are you? He asked.

What's your name? He asked again.

Mister's voice is a wave of warmth on a cold winter day, yet it was piercing at the same time. How could such a tender voice be associated with politics that leave nothing but death in its wake? May Mister be a teacher in his next life so he could use that voice of his to read poetry to his students. May he no longer be involved in mind games and set-ups, but be able to start a family of his own and live a normal life. Maybe he'll have a grand wedding, or maybe the two of them will choose to settle down in the depths of a forest on a beautiful mountain. They will probably give birth to three children, two boys, and one girl so the boys will protect the girl whenever she needs help. Maybe they'll never have children, and it'll just be the two of them forever.

How great would that be? Miss Liu thought.

Liu, fifteen.

He mouthed her name one more time, the sudden burst of affection in his eyes made it seem like he was about to utter something else. He let out a breath, took his left hand out and waved it slightly, then placed his pipe between his body and his arm. He took off a glove, and right there in front of her were his pale wrist, his long, slim fingers, and fingertips that were as red as hers.

This is bad, right?

***

Ben Xi Municipal Tax Bureau, director's office.

Hei Shan sat properly behind his desk, his old leather shoes blending into the wooden floor. He had bushy eyebrows and dark skin due to the sun. He played with his pen between his fingers. He had horrible handwriting, his characters were so messy they looked like A Dao's work.

The girl in front of him had just graduated high school. Her waist-long braid swung back and forth as she spoke, hypnotizing Hei Shan. Pretty, so pretty.

Name? Hei Shan asked.

Wu Yang.

Not bad. A Hui?

Yes.

Nice handwriting.

Thank you.

Why do you want to be my secretary?

Just because.

The first thing Hei Shan said when he got home later that day was, dad, I'm getting married. Hei Shan's father was yawning, and pulling himself together after a great nap, when he heard Hei Shan's mother yell from the kitchen, choose a date!

Hei Shan grabbed his canvas bag and yanked it away from his shoulders, then pulled out a chair and sat down. His father slowly sat down next to him, shuffling two stone beads with one hand, and staring at his son. True, Hei Shan's already twenty-one, he should be interested in girls by now. Hei Shan was an awkward young man, which explains why his father had been really worried about the family line being cut off from his generation. Hei Shan's father had introduced many suitable girls to him in the past few years, but he liked none of them. Finally, his father thought, finally he has found the one.

After asking some serious questions, Hei Shan's father was able to paint a faint image of Wu Yang in his mind. She was also a Hui, good-looking, and educated. It almost sounded too good to be true, so when Hei Shan told his father to go and ask for permission from her family, his father immediately said yes.

Wu Yang's father was much more straightforward than what Hei Shan's father had expected. Her father was charming and carried himself with great composure. In the beginning, Hei Shan's father was worried that his future in-law might be a condescending, stuck up man. Once he met him, he realized that his imagination had him fooled. Not only was Wu Yang's father extremely welcoming, the two also shared some similar interests.

Hei Shan's father was really into tea, and it wasn't like he had anything else to do with all that free time. When Wu Yang's father showed him his tea collection, he instantly saw the tin of Long Jing he had been searching for everywhere. Her father was a businessman, so he knew exactly what to do. He took the Long Jing off from its shelf and began warming up the teapot and teacups. He took occasional glances at Hei Shan's father, whose concentration was on his hands, and filled his own mind with thoughts.

This man sitting right in front of me seems decent so his son won't be far off. Plus, he works for the government, which means that if Hei Shan and Wu Yang do get married, she will be comfortable for the rest of her life. As to whether she wants this or not, well, it really depends on what Hei Shan is willing to do for her since she's not an easy girl.

A few cups of tea later, the two fathers smiled and shook each other's hand after they had finally reached an agreement.

three

1949, the establishment of government in People's Republic of China.

The Hui restaurant next to the Lius was crowded, as usual, and so was the Liu house.

The servants brought out dishes and

bowls one by one, their footsteps so fast they made you dizzy. Master Liu sat in the middle of the feast with Mrs. Liu, née Ding, and Miss Liu on either side of him. The other children talked away, and the room was filled with laughter. The girls talked about new clothes and new shoes. The oldest son had just begun asking Master Liu questions about starting a business when Master Liu cut him off with, you'll only lose money. The second oldest son was reading a book on *Political Economy* and constantly fixing his glasses that kept sliding off the bridge of his nose. The third oldest son, who was

sitting the furthest away from Master Liu,
kept knocking on the table. There was no
doubt that he had run out of money again.
There were three empty seats for Master
Liu's three other children. He said that even
though they're gone at a young age, we
can't erase their traces from our lives. They
were family.

Miss Liu didn't like the noise, let
alone the meaningless chatter. She put her
chopsticks down and left. The others seemed
used to this situation. They knew that Miss
Liu was going to do whatever she wanted.

Miss Liu had a closet made out of high-quality incense wood in her room, which took Master Liu a lot of effort to bring home from Yunnan. Apparently, it could make clothes smell like different kinds of flowers. At first, Miss Liu didn't want it at all. It was huge, so it took up space, and it had a weird odor that kept giving her headaches. But one day, on her way home from school, Miss Liu saw servants moving it out, so she ran in front of them and hugged the closet, refusing to let go. The servants were a bit confused, but they couldn't move it anymore, so it stayed.

There was a mahogany box with a lock on it in the closet that had been there the whole time. It was only discovered a few months after the closet had been delivered. It was probably a surprise from the carpenter since it was covered with delicately carved patterns. Originally, Miss Liu wanted to give it to her mother as a gift, since Mrs. Liu, n é e Ding, liked to put her jewelry in mahogany boxes. She said they made jewelry seem more precious and made her more respectable, but Miss Liu never gave her the box.

It was a box full of love.

Dear Lan,

How are you today?

I saw you yesterday and wanted to talk to you, but you seemed tired so I stayed back. You haven't been resting well, have you? I know that you're busy with school, but I didn't expect it to be this exhausting. Ever since I saw you the other day, I can't stop thinking about you. Forgive me for being so straightforward, but I just can't control myself. The weather's chilly, remember to drink a lot of hot water so your stomach won't hurt and you won't catch a cold. If you don't mind, there's a small restaurant right across from your school where you can visit every now and then. I'd be lying if I said I'm not being selfish, but I really want you to try some of their sugar pancakes. I heard some people say that most girls like sweets, do you?

Hope you're well.

Dear Lan,

How are you today?

I remember promising a few days ago that I would take you out for a walk near the lake. When are you free? I know that your father's strict, so it's fine if you can't make it. It's just that I haven't seen you for a while, and I miss you. The hardest time is over, so lately I've been a little distracted, writing poems just to pass time. I want to give you a few poems that I've written the next time we meet, one, for your feedback, and two, so that you'll be thinking of me as well. I'll be waiting for a response.

Hope you're well.

Dear Lan,

How are you today?

I walked past your house this morning and saw several branches of flowering plums in your yard. You said they represent improvement and the desire to better oneself. I don't know much about flowers, but I'm sure that you're right. I'm thinking about planting some near my place so we can improve together. I also want to find a space where I can plant a lot more of them, and we can go next year during April or May when they bloom. What do you think?

Hope you're well.

***

Winter, 1951.

Hei Shan woke up earlier than A Dao. He jumped off his kang, and hurried outside to the public bathroom, slamming the door behind him. The loud noise woke his parents up.

Hei Shan's father was just about to head out and give his son a good beating when his wife pulled him back. He mumbled something to himself then went back to sleep. Hei Shan's mother, on the other hand, couldn't sleep anymore. It was a big day, she had to cook a delicious breakfast to cheer her son up. As she was trying to decide what to make, Hei Shan's mother heard their next door neighbor Aunt Zhang's resonant voice.

Aunt Zhang was nice and welcoming. She was willing to lend a hand whenever the Heis needed help. She knew they were Huis, so she made sure that when they came to visit, nothing with pork was ever on the table. However, her warmth wasn't just for maintaining a good relationship between neighbors, but also for her niece, who was a fair, young girl with a crush on Hei Shan ever since she was little. Aunt Zhang would frequently chat with Hei Shan's mother, just to set the two of them up. She even figured out whose house they would visit first during New Years after they get married.

Hei Shan's mother liked Aunt Zhang, and she had nothing against her niece, but something seemed to be missing, so she would always avoid these conversations and talk about something else. As time went by, Aunt Zhang eventually realized that her niece was the only one who wanted to take things to the next level, so she stopped bringing it up. But on that day, for some reason, Aunt Zhang happened to find out about what was going on.

Although Hei Shan's mother and Aunt Zhang didn't end their conversation on a high note, Hei Shan's mother was still glad that she had straightened things out. She knew what a loveless marriage looked like because if it wasn't for Hei Shan's father, she would've been trapped in one as well. But she was still a mother, so she couldn't help but feel sorry for Aunt Zhang's niece. The girl gave her whole heart but got nothing in return.

Aunt Zhang's niece later married the son of an important government official. He was temperamental and violent. Aunt Zhang's niece went to look for Hei Shan before he headed out the other day. People always say that those who are close to death will have a sudden burst of energy before they collapse, which also describes her love for Hei Shan. When a young girl of the perfect age meets a man who seems to be the one, there's really no reason for her to turn away and look for something else. If she could, of course, she would've waited for

him. He was like the Sun, out of reach, but

too bright to ignore. Yet the thing about love

is that it has the power to make the most

stubborn choose to leave.

  She was shy and wasn't good at

speaking, not the type of girl Hei Shan liked.

She knew that, but she didn't want to be

weak anymore. She wanted to try for the last

time, so when she looks back at her teenage

years, she won't feel as if she didn't give

herself closure. She prepared a long speech

but was too afraid to say it in front of him.

She was afraid of being rejected, and of

being erased from his life forever.

Her last memory of Hei Shan was a brief smile. He was such an outgoing person, but when it came to her, he had always been distant. Look, he's going to meet the girl of his dreams, don't take his politeness as a sign to keep going. Apart from wishing him good luck, there really wasn't anything else she could do. Be careful, she said. Although her last word, along with her last glimmer of hope, were both carried away by the gust of wind he left behind.

It was painful, but it was worth her time.

Aunt Zhang's niece died not long after she married the government official's son, while her husband married a girl he grew up with right after. Even her spirit tablet was never put in his ancestral hall.

The young and beautiful wind up living a short life.

After Hei Shan came back from the public bathroom, he borrowed his mother's mirror and took a careful look at himself. He was a handsome young man, but he didn't seem to be satisfied by what he saw. He felt like the bags under his eyes were too big, which made him look like a panda. He also disliked the redness in his eyes, which seemed to indicate insomnia and poor renal function. Anyway, Hei Shan's morning was accompanied by A Dao's barking, his mother's nagging, and his own heart beating.

It was his first date with Wu Yang.

Hei Shan's father had said that girls liked shopping. Having zero experience with dating, Hei Shan had no choice but to listen to his father. Hei Shan's family didn't have a lot of money. He tried to save up so the two of them could take the tram, but it wasn't enough. Hei Shan then thought about taking Wu Yang out for a nice walk. Walking's similar to shopping, right?

Wu Yang ended up paying for the tram tickets, which made her seem even greater in Hei Shan's eyes. He had never met a girl like her. She was quiet and sometimes appeared to be cold, very different from the other girls Hei Shan's father had set him up with before. Nothing seemed to catch her attention, in fact, Hei Shan was worried that her eyes might be polluted by the mundaneness of her surroundings. When those eyes rested on objects as ordinary as a flower or a tree, Hei Shan swore he could see them change, but he didn't know why. That was when Hei Shan told himself when I become rich, the first thing I'm going to do is marry her.

four

Miss Liu started smoking when she was sixteen years old.

Her mother would scold her, saying that a Hui girl should not be carrying a pipe around all day, it makes you look cheap. Miss Liu didn't care, and she would continue huffing and puffing as her mother searched for something to drink after giving another long and tedious lecture.

Miss Liu learned how to smoke that winter. It probably had a lot to do with the first time she met Mister, because ever since then, whenever it snowed, Miss Liu would sit on her kang with a pipe in one hand, and facing the window, breathe out toward the falling snowflakes. She was beautiful when she smoked. Her quivering eyelashes and rosy cheeks were signs of internal struggles and deep thoughts. She was probably the only one who could smoke so elegantly.

They all said that Miss Liu was smart and caring, whoever gets to marry her in the future should be laughing their head off. But when she was alone, Miss Liu always wondered how she would be like if she were a man. She would be highly educated, good—looking, but not faithful. No matter how many women fall for her, she would never even bat an eye, and no one would shame her, because she would be a knowledgeable and respectable man. As for those women, they'd only become jokes she would tell at the dinner table.

Miss Liu had stopped receiving Mister's letters for the past few days. She knew exactly how her father felt about him, but confronting Mr. Liu meant never seeing Mister again. She wanted to keep her composure, but being in love can make anyone a fool. Mr. Liu had been trying to prevent the two from seeing each other, but Miss Liu wasn't going to back down. After another failed attempt to escape, her father couldn't take it anymore.

Mr. Liu wasn't a strict father, but he knew what was going on. Miss Liu's sneaking around wasn't news to him. The reason why he didn't immediately ground her was that he was curious. What kind of person could make his daughter fall so hard?

Of course, Mr. Liu was overprotective, just like any other parent. Although sixteen was an appropriate age for dating, he just didn't like how mysterious Mister was. When he found out that Mister was a Han, he knew for sure that the romance between Mister and his daughter definitely had to come to an end.

The alley where Mister lived was their secret garden. Although it was quite a walk from the Liu house, Miss Liu didn't care. Her mother had told her about two different kinds of love. The first kind is intense and passionate. When you fall in love with someone, you'd do anything for them. But the second kind is calm and steady, like a flowing river. It's cooking, fighting, and forgiving. You'll probably want the first kind because it's once in a lifetime, but it won't last.

As a girl, if you want the rest of your life to be free of trouble, you should choose the second kind.

Miss Liu thought about her mother's

words a lot, then all that would be left was disdain. She knew she was different ever since she was born. She was the most beautiful rose in the garden, but she also had the most thorns. She believed that love itself should be memorable, even if the promise of a future was nowhere to be seen. At least later, when she would reflect upon her youth, she wouldn't regret anything.

Miss Liu loved watching Mister smoke. She couldn't understand why she never felt annoyed when a column of smoke would creep around the two of them. Mister would sometimes lower his body, position his head right next to her ear, and let out a deep breath. His unconscious moves would make her heart pound faster than ever.

He was mesmerizing.

Miss Liu said she also wanted to smoke, but he said no. She asked him why, and Mister simply said that it was bad for her health. He then asked her why she liked such bizarre things, so Miss Liu, in all seriousness, began listing all of the things she disliked one by one. She disliked a lot of things, so many he had lost count.

Will you stop liking me?

That's stupid, I only like you.

Mister said that if it was possible, he wanted to die on the front line because that was the closest he could be from his belief. He didn't want to use only his mind for a living. His patience had already been worn out by doing the same things repeatedly, never catching a break. The scheming and calculating can go to hell! All that he ever wanted to do was to hold a gun.

Mister died in the fall of 1949.

Dead leaves that were tinted yellow landed on his head and his body, becoming the only color he was wearing. He never got the chance to plant the flowering plums or wait until the next summer when they would bloom. He didn't die on the front line as he had wished, and when he looked around for the last time, he saw brick houses lined up unevenly, he saw moving heads hovering over him, but he didn't see Miss Liu. After the crowd left, he was all alone. He was a clean man, yet he lay there, motionless, lifeless, buried in the mud and the softly blowing wind.

Miss Liu had really thought about marrying him, and she sincerely believed that he had wanted that as well.

***

1958, Hei Shan was twenty-eight, Wu Yang twenty-five.

Wu Yang's father's clinic had established a public-private partnership with the Chinese government. His vouchers became invalid, so he became an unoccupied

man who made eight hundred RMB a month.
He didn't like the thought of giving up his
clinic since it took him years to build it. It
was hard for him to let go. He eventually
realized that the money he had made was
going to last him and his family a long time,
and came to terms with the fact that his body
no longer functioned like it used to before. It
was time for him to take a break. He thought
Wu Yang was going to stay by his side and
take care of him, but he didn't expect her
and Hei Shan to move to Ningxia only a few
years after they got married.

Before that, Wu Yang was a working woman. She left the city she was born in after she married Hei Shan, and brought her father with them when they moved to Changchun. She was a film editor at Changchun Film Studio. She had edited many pieces, including the famous *The Great River Flows On*. Wu Yang chose this job for a reason. She was extremely interested in the love stories and could memorize most of the lines, but she would always deny it and say she forgot whenever someone asked. There was never really a reason why Wu Yang refused to show off her film knowledge, but no one could force her to do anything. She simply liked watching the lives of other people from an onlooker's perspective.

Wu Yang's life drastically changed after Hei Shan became the Chief of the Communications Division and the two of them moved to Ningxia. She couldn't find another job similar to the one she had before, but Wu Yang wasn't going to give up. Soon, she entered the Ningxia Opera Troupe and became a personnel cadre.

The more operas she saw, the clearer it seemed to Wu Yang that operas and films were the same. They both tell stories. Their biggest difference, however, is that film actors know that they're acting, while opera singers become one with their role. Wu Yang would always think, was Yu Ji's sword dance really for Xiang Yu, or was it for herself? When she said his name one last time, was it because she had made a decision, or just her heart shattering into a million pieces? Even a warrior like Xiang Yu chose to kill himself after surviving the war just to reunite with the love of his life. It was apparent that no matter who you are, you shouldn't lose the one thing you consider to be the most important, whether it's a possession or a beauty.

Wu Yang was still happy after being through everything. Hei Shan took great care of her, and he gave her all the support he could possibly give. If Wu Yang felt tired when they were outside with friends, Hei Shan would immediately pay for the entire meal and take her home. Some acquaintances of his would always complain about him losing his freedom after getting married, but Hei Shan never bothered to argue with them. They didn't understand a thing about the life the two of them shared.

Although Hei Shan wasn't as knowledgeable as Wu Yang when it came to art appreciation, he still tried very hard just so they could have a deep conversation every now and then. He bought loads and loads of books on the history of Beijing Opera and filled them with notes. Hei Shan sometimes wondered where Wu Yang's thoughts came from. He had never seen her read books on philosophy, yet her mind seemed to be full of profound ideas he had never even heard of. The more Hei Shan tried to keep up with her, the more evident it became to him that

Wu Yang was so special, he wasn't going to meet another person anywhere close to her.

Wu Yang was smart, indeed, but she was also used to being the daughter of a prestigious family. She didn't know how to do chores at all. All she would do at home was to eat sunflower seeds and play Mah Jong. She became so good, even the head of the Ningxia Opera Troupe who had been playing for decades, admitted defeat.

The first thing Wu Yang did each morning was to drink tea, and it had to be a cup of warm highland barley. As the Chief of the Communications Division, Hei Shan always came home bearing gifts from those who wanted to impress him. Wu Yang hated their gifts, especially the kinds of tea leaves that could be seen anywhere on the streets. She didn' t want to be just like everyone else, and that was what Hei Shan loved about her, and the reason why he would always wake up before she did and make her a cup of tea at the perfect temperature.

Wu Yang had imagined a life like this since she was a child.

five

Miss Liu turned eighteen at the beginning of 1951.

Her second oldest sister died from pulmonary tuberculosis.

She asked Master Liu multiple times why he refused to treat his own daughter. No matter how she posed the question, his only response was because your sister is already married. It's quite ironic, she thought. Her sister was a Liu so naturally. she had a grand wedding. Miss Liu vaguely recalled the night before her sister's wedding when the two of them shared true thoughts and feelings they had never shared before. Her sister kept reminding her to take care of their mother and mentioned a bit of everyone else in the family as well. Miss Liu kept nodding her head as she carefully observed her sister's expression. She didn't look like a bride to be.

Sister.

Hm?

Do you love him?

Her sister said the man she was about to marry came from a good family and he was highly educated. She said she got lucky. Plus, love didn't matter. It was just a concept that you won't be able to carry with you into the grave anyway. Miss Liu could see her vulnerability under all that wisdom. Her sister was crying and the tears were not happy.

Her sister knew equality was something out of reach. She really envied Miss Liu. Her youngest sister had always been cared for by their father and everyone else in the family. Apart from their brothers, Miss Liu was the only girl Master Liu still took care of. He would hold her hand and call her by the nickname he gave her when she was little. Her sister simply took his obvious favoritism as a sign of concern. It made her feel better.

The day of her wedding, she put on a full

face of makeup and disguise. No one could tell how she really felt, they all assumed that she was having the greatest time of her life. The bright red decorations made her face glow. Any girl who saw her wedding would've been jealous to the core.

Miss Liu remembered the day when her sister and her husband went to the ward office. She remembered her sister's expression. Her face went from hopeful to hopeless. When Miss Liu watched the two of them bowing to each other, she finally realized something.

The thing about love is that it always

attacks you when you least expect it.

Miss Liu had met the boy once when her sister was teaching her needlework so she could make something for Mister. He died before she finished it.

The boy was holding a pot of some unknown succulent. He had a decent appearance and seemed to be the type of person who you could trust. Miss Liu felt like he would' ve been there to listen to all her complaints. Her sister had most likely become interested in plants and flowers because of him. Oh right, his name was A

Liu, also a Hui. He came from a middle-class family and his father was a teacher. Miss Liu had probably seen his father at school. A Liu disappeared on the day her sister got married. It didn't matter if he enlisted or moved away, the two of them were never going to see each other again.

Humans are weird. We always think that the best things are the ones we can't have.

Miss Liu realized something on the day of her sister's funeral. You could be rich or poor, respected or despised, but death will eventually take everything away from you and leave you with nothing. Her sister left behind her favorite cloth shoes, her most treasured jade bracelet, and her husband who soon married someone else.

Her sister' s husband wasn' t a perfect man, but Miss Liu felt sorry for him. Maybe because the two of them had much in common, Miss Liu even read a poem she wrote on his other wedding. The poem was about how she hoped that the newlyweds would stay together forever. She hoped that another person would be able to give him what her sister couldn't. His life had been changed after her sister's death, and she knew that their marriage took a toll on him as well.

Miss Liu talked about a lot with him on the day of his wedding.

Hey little sister, listen. When we got married, she was twenty-three, I was twenty-nine, we were six years apart. She was twenty-four when she left, and I was thirty. Now I'm thirty-two, married again, and she's still twenty-four. She'd be twenty-four when I become a father, twenty—four when I become a grandfather,

twenty—four if I ever get a chance to

become a great—grandfather. I' ll probably

be seventy or eighty by the time I die, and

she' d still be twenty—four.

Twenty—four represents a youthful age

and an everlasting beauty, the only things

that' ll come to mind when you think of her.

The weather was still cold at the

beginning of the year, sending shivers down

your spine. The Chinese rose her sister had

planted only showed signs of blooming on

the day she died, and became fully bloomed on the day of her funeral.

* * *

Wu Yang's mother died when she was twenty-seven.

That same year, she gave birth to her first daughter.

Wu Yang's daughter gave her solace. As a new mother, she was unfamiliar with everything. She had hoped that her own mother would be there to help her, but destiny makes a fool out of everyone. Wu Yang's mother didn't suffer, which made Wu Yang blame herself even more. She had always felt like she owed her mother a lot. She made her worry too much during her teenage years, which was probably the reason why her mother's health went on a downward spiral after she grew old. Wu Yang had promised her family that she would take good care of her mother, but she couldn't keep her.

Wu Yang's head was filled with words from somebody who had already passed away. Words she spoke to Wu Yang while holding her hands. Words that conveyed the thoughts and feelings they had never shared before.

We don't bring anything into or out of this world. After we've had our chance at seeing the beauty of it all, whether it be satisfying or regretful, at least we had the journey.

Wu Yang would think of these words as she collected her mother's belongings. They made her feel at peace.

Her daughter's crying would always help her pull herself together. Life goes on no matter what. Although Wu Yang wasn't used to the tiring reality of childcare, she tried her best to raise her daughter the way her mother had raised her. Wu Yang believed that if her mother could raise a girl like her who didn't seem to fit in anywhere, yet had a soul that was both profound and interesting, she could too.

Sometimes, at night, when she would put her daughter to sleep, Wu Yang swore she could see her mother's figure inside the child's clear, bright eyes.

Wu Yang's father died when she was

thirty-six.

The same year, she gave birth to her second daughter.

Before he died, Wu Yang's father gave her a pair of cotton gloves with an eight hundred RMB savings book inside them. The cunning old fellow, without surprise, remembered to leave something behind for his favorite daughter.

Her father told her a lot of stories about her teenage years. He said he felt sorry. Even though Wu Yang had her own family and a stable job, he couldn't forget how hysteric she was in the old Liu house. He could see it whenever he closed his eyes. Whenever Wu Yang heard that, she would try to brush past the subject by saying everything was over. She knew best if it was over or not. You don't just forget about what happened during your teenage years, but Wu Yang had convinced herself that nothing was perfect. The cleanest things become dusty and unrecognizable if you give them time.

Wu Yang was a lot calmer when she faced her father's death. Her first daughter had already turned nine and could entertain herself most of the time. Her second daughter was still a newborn but she rarely cried. The two of them allowed Wu Yang to prepare for her father's funeral without any distraction.

Her father's death marked the end of the first half of Wu Yang's life. It not only took away her last thoughts about her old house but also the knot that had been inside her heart for all these years.

From that day on, Wu Yang's first eighteen years seemed to her like the films she had edited. Far, far away.

six

Hei Shan died when he was sixty–seven.

They all said that he lived a life without regrets. He married a beautiful Hui woman and became the father of two sensible and intelligent girls.

Hei Shan seemed to know that he was

dying so he took care of everything before he left. His two daughters who were both married didn't know anything about his condition. They saw him laugh and joke every day, looking nothing like a sick person. Hei Shan's only regret was that he never got to hold his second daughter's baby, his granddaughter. Apart from that, there was nothing else he still wanted in his ordinary life. Hei Shan said a lot to Wu Yang before he left, I won't go into detail. You could guess that he definitely said his goodbye properly to the woman who had been holding his love and affection for decades.

Thinking back at the things he did and the people he's met, the word ordinary seems to sum it all up. An ordinary background, an ordinary first love, an ordinary family, and an ordinary departure. But it was a person who was so ordinary that could pour his whole heart out and expect nothing in return. He knew that life was short, and it was only enough for him to cherish the people he cherished. He never complained about the fleeting time, because sixty-seven years were enough for him to figure out how to use it wisely. He was happy because those he cared about were happy, and he was willing to bear the pain in their place.

His never lived his life for himself.

His two daughters who could take care of everything by then made sure Hei Shan left with dignity and respect. They also paid attention to Wu Yang's feelings, but she would always tell the kids to go and do what they had to do. She said that she was old and that they were too noisy for her to handle. That was a lie. The best thing Wu Yang could think of was her daughters joking around right next to her. She just didn't know how to cope with the sudden loss after being strong for all this time. She had lost a lot of things in her life, and she assumed that she was skilled at such an extreme sport. Wu Yang didn't expect that, after all these years, she would still be able to feel the pain she felt the first time she lost something, even sharper.

Hei Shan was born into this world with nothing, but he took away all of Wu Yang's love when he left.

Wu Yang hadn't smoked in years. It was on the day Hei Shan left when she bought a pack of cigarettes without letting the kids know. She lit the cigarette awkwardly, then put the other end in her mouth, between her teeth.

Time has changed a lot of things. From war to peace, Wu Yang had been through it all. She saw everything she knew being overthrown then rebuilt. The only thing that hadn't changed was her wish to keep moving forward. She wanted to keep up with the times and the changes in her heart.

She liked not using pipes. She found

them heavy anyway, now everything's nice
and easy.

That night, Wu Yang didn't feel weird
lying in the bed by herself. She was just a
bit annoyed by the smell of cigarettes that
had taken over her nostrils. Hei Shan used
to say that women shouldn't smoke, they
should smell sweet and be taken care of by
men every day. Wu Yang had a big fight with
him and Hei Shan was so scared he just kept
apologizing. Hei Shan could never be the
man of the house in front of Wu Yang, he
was simply a caring husband. Thinking about

it now, she found her old self to be kind of hilarious. Of course she knew of Hei Shan's intent. The heart that had always wanted to please her could never be hidden.

Wu Yang had told herself many times that it was okay to cry. Don't panic, Hei Shan had simply gone to a better place. He was too tired, so you have to learn to let go and say goodbye to him with a smile on your face. You have to tell him everything will be fine because I'll be here. But the Sun will rise again and night will fall as well. You need to think of him when you're feeling helpless and tell yourself that you will continue living as if he was still here. When that look has seeped into your skin, mixed with your blood, and sunk to your bones that will eventually look like his, yes, you will become one with it. But after that, you need to start a new life. You need to keep eating sunflower seeds and playing Mah Jong. You will watch the sun rise and set as well.

She told herself that you need to live better than you did before because he's waiting for you. He's waiting for the days you will share together after the dust settles.

seven

Mom, was it love at first sight between you and dad?

He was good-looking but his family was too poor.

Mom, did you have a first love?

No.

Hei Shan laughed. How come? There was a very handsome Kuomintang officer who pursued your mother.

Why didn't the Kuomintang work out? Where did the man go?

I don't know.

Hei Shan laughed again. Where do you think he went?

Did he retreat to Taiwan? Or was he captured?

He was executed.

Mom, your name is Wu Yang, but my

grandfather's last name is Liu. Why isn't

your full name Liu Wu Yang?

There are too many Lius out there.

I don't want to be like everyone else.

图书在版编目（CIP）数据

刘小姐：汉、英 / 法图麦·李著 .— 武汉：长江文艺出版社，
2018.11

ISBN 978-7-5702-0696-4

I. ①刘… II. ①法… III. ①短篇小说 – 中国 – 当代 – 汉、英 IV. ① I247.7

中国版本图书馆 CIP 数据核字 (2018) 第 244684 号

刘小姐

法图麦·李　著

选题产品策划生产机构 | 北京长江新世纪文化传媒有限公司

总 策 划 | 金丽红　黎　波　安波舜

策划编辑 | 张　维

责任编辑 | 张　维　　　　装帧设计 | 郭　璐　　　　媒体运营 | 刘　冲　刘　峥

法律顾问 | 张艳萍　　　　内文制作 | 张景莹　　　　责任印制 | 张志杰　王会利

版权代理 | 何　红

总 发 行 | 北京长江新世纪文化传媒有限公司

电　　话 | 010-58678881　　　　　　　　　　传　　真 | 010-58677346

地　　址 | 北京市朝阳区曙光西里甲 6 号时间国际大厦 A 座 1905 室　　　邮　　编 | 100028

出　　版 | 长江出版传媒　长江文艺出版社

地　　址 | 湖北省武汉市雄楚大街 268 号湖北出版文化城 B 座 9–11 楼　　　邮　　编 | 430070

印　　刷 | 三河市兴博印务有限公司

开　　本 | 787 毫米 ×1092 毫米　1/32　　　　印　　张 | 5.625

版　　次 | 2018 年 11 月第 1 版　　　　　　　印　　次 | 2018 年 11 月第 1 次印刷

字　　数 | 52 千字

定　　价 | 45.00 元

盗版必究（举报电话：010-58678881）

（图书如出现印装质量问题，请与选题产品策划生产机构联系调换）